THE TIME WASTE IS LIFE WASTE

THE TIME WASTE IS LIFE WASTE

A. SHASHANK

A nation's prosperity is dependent on how people use their time in the performance of good actions. The challenge for humanity is lack of clarity, motivation and laziness. You may be intelligent, but if you do not act nothing is going to happen. This denies us the ability to offer our gifts to the world. Time wasted is Life wasted says Bhagawan Sri Sathya Sai.

"Also, examine the usage of time. One should not waste time. Time should be spent in a useful manner. Time should be sanctified because everything in this creation is dependent on time. Even our scriptures extol God as 'Kaalaya namaha. Kaalaatheethaya namaha (Salutations to the One who is the embodiment of Time and who transcends Time).'" – Sathya Sai

"Time is an essential part of our life. Do not defile time by gossiping and unnecessary talk. The truth behind the saying "Don't waste time" is that no time should be wasted in evil thoughts and acts. Instead, make use of time in an efficient way." – Sathya Sai

Time Management: In order to accomplish the task of bringing your future into the present, you need the correct thoughts, vision and motivation. That is why Kala Bhairava remains one of the most powerful beings in the world. Kala Bhairava, The Lord of Time, will not only show you the Vision of what it is you want to create, but he will also give you the exact knowledge and clarity of how to get it. This new profound knowledge gives you no other choice but to take action now to follow your dreams.

When was the last time you woke up in the morning being clear, motivated and happy, knowing exactly how to implement your dreams immediately?

You need clarity within your own mind for creation. And you need to be motivated to act. When you do nothing, little changes and your dreams remain in your imagination, never to be given to the world.

The Power of Time: Master Time with 8 Powerful Keepers of Time and Action: There is nothing more precious than your time and once it is spent, it is gone forever. Lord Kala Bhairava who is a manifestation of Lord Shiva oversees the march of time and draws you to specific locations. By accessing the energy of Kala Bhairava, you completely take charge of the moments in your life and avoid future delays, lethargy and unfortunate events.

How to Unleash the Power of Bhairava to Make Your Dreams a Real, Now?

Bhairava can force you to jump over the bad time choices you make in the form of laziness, lethargy and idleness. You must also obtain the consciousness to discontinue unrewarding action, in your own job.

-A.Shashank

Contents

Foreword

The saying that "time and tide wait for no man" means different things to different people. To some, it is precious and important while to many others, it is common and available when the need arises. The right essence of time is really in the doing and not in the waiting. A time spent in doing something worthwhile always comes back fruitfully. What cannot be allocated time is indeed not worth doing. Certainly, a person who invests time reading and writing is expected to acquire sound knowledge and writing skills. Time is life. He who wastes time has not only wasted life, but has also injured eternity. A person who wastes time in doing nothing will eventually end up being nothing. There is no two ways about that.

Sincerely speaking, a lot depends on the good use of time. Time used judiciously in reading and writing will eventually make one educated, knowledgeable and skilful. Famous scholars and writers like Les Brown, John Mason, Wole Soyinka, Kevin Hogan, Chimamanda Adichie, to mention but a few, are what they are today because they invested so much with their time. It goes without saying that good time management is always rewarding and self-fulfilling.

Worthy to note, time is the currency of the world. Anything one devotes much time doing largely determines what one is going to be in the future. If one decides to spend most of one's time in running, one will certainly become a good athlete. Again, if one spends one's time in dancing, one will definitely become a good dancer. There is time for everything. There is time to work and play. There is time to read, socialise and to sleep, everything has its own time allocation. When one uses the time for reading to sleep, one abuses that particular time. When one does the right thing at the right time, one manages time effectively. The end result is always rewarding and result-oriented.

Whether fleeting or standstill, time goes around and fails to come around. Time wasted can never be regained. Invest time now and not later.

-A.Shashank

Preface

It was the book Mainly Written For Children's to understand the value of time. Children Should understant Stand Time is More than Money.Time is precious than a diamond or Money. Many of the Children Used To waste their time by Watching Mobile Or Telivision. So I took This Topic "Time Wate is Life Waste". It took 3Months To Research and complete the book.

-A.Shashank

Acknowledgements

The Negative Effect of Smartphones on Child Development:

The drawbacks of smartphone use on children has received attention in recent years. In academia, journalism, and other popular forms of media, there has been a growing concern for the ways that children have increased access to smartphone technology.

Specifically, the behavioral consequences of smartphone dependency in children has received the attention of scholars across the world. An article titled "Association between mobile technology use and child adjustment in early elementary school age" used data compiled from a group of 1,642 first-grade children in Japan to determine whether there's a link between the use of smartphone technology and behavioral development. The researchers found that "routine and frequent use of mobile devices appear to be associated with behavioral problems in childhood."

Additionally, some scholars have even turned toward the adverse bodily effects that smartphones can have on children. A recent article published in the journal Child Development explored the physical health consequences of smartphone use for children. It stated that, as more children begin using smartphones at earlier ages, "it is of importance that neurological diseases, physiological addiction, cognition, sleep and behavioral problems are considered." Because of this, parents and clinicians should be aware of the repercussions of early-age smartphone usage.

The Mobile Phones are one of the Example of Time Waste.

A Kid Using a Tablet

-A.Shashank

Prologue

Effective Utilization of Time

For effectively utilizing the time we must consider some points which will help us in our whole life. This utilization includes setting goals, prepare work lists, prioritize task, and take adequate sleep and various others.

For effectively utilizing time set long and short term goals these goals will help you in remaining productive. Moreover, they will prove as a driving force that will keep you motivated. Also, this will give the willingness to achieve something in life.

In the beginning, it will feel like a boring task but when you do it regularly then you will realize that that it only helps you to increase your productivity. Ultimately, this will force you to achieve more in life.

Prioritizing task is a very effective way of managing time. Also, because of it, you will know the importance of various task and jobs. Apart from that, if your club and perform a similar activity in a go then it also increases your productivity. Hence, it will help you to achieve more in life.

Being productive does not mean that you engage yourself in different tasks every time. Taking proper sleep and exercising is also part of being productive. Besides, proper exercise and sleep maintain a balance between body and mind which is very important for being productive and efficient.Value of Time

Although most people do not understand how valuable time is until they lost it. Besides, there are people in the world who prioritize money over time because according to them, time is nothing. But, they do not realize the fact that it is time that has given them the opportunity to earn money. Apart from this, the time has given us prosperity and happiness and on the contrary, it has also given us sorrow and grief.

-A.Shashank

1

Time Waste is Life Waste

Time Waste is a Big Blunder

Time is the embodiment of God. Hence Time is called Samvatsara (year). The sages have described God as Kaalaroopaaya (the embodiment of Time). All things in the Cosmos, moving and unmoving, are permeated by God. Hence, God is characterised as Kaalagarbha (the One who holds Time in the womb). Sages have also described Him as Dheerothama (Supreme among the valiant). The term Dheera should not be understood as meaning one who is a great intellectual or highly intelligent person. Dheera is the appellation given by the Veda to a man who turns his Dhee (intelligence) towards God. The word Kaalam (Time) is derived from Kaa+alam. This means that God, embodiment of Time, is the One who rewards people according to their deservedness. God does not submit to worldly offerings, worldly authority or worldly power. He responds only to spiritual aspirations.

Realise the true goal of your life:

In the world, we are continually experiencing the same round of days and nights. You perform the same ablutions and indulge in the same process of filling the stomach. Thus you go on from year to year. But what efforts are you making to lead a purposeful and ennobling life? You are going through the same mill of experiences again and again, doing the same things again and again. If you go on in this way, what is the worth of your life? What is the goal of life? What is its primary purpose? Few care to enquire into this basic question.

Hence what we have to examine is how we can lead an ideal, bliss-filled, spiritually-oriented life which will serve as an example to others. People are engaged in Sadhana. But when the outcome of these exercises is examined, it is found to be without meaning. All these exercises are purely designed to provide some sort of mental satisfaction and nothing more.

In my view, neither Sadhana (spiritual endeavour) nor Sadhyam (fulfillment) exists independently and apart from each other. Sadhana and Sadhyam are one and the same. It is a trick of the mind to make Sadhana as the means to Sadhyam (the Goal). True Sadhana consists in giving up the Anaatma bhava (the idea that one is not the Spirit but the physical body). To turn the vision from the physical to the spiritual constitutes real Sadhana.

Today, we have knowledge of many sorts in the world. All these categories of knowledge do not constitute what is regarded as Jnana in Vedantic parlance. Atma Jnana (knowledge of the Spirit) alone is true knowledge. Ordinary knowledge may be knowledge of material objects, sensory knowledge, or any other kind of knowledge acquired by investigation. But none of these can be Atma Jnana. In the highest sense Atma (the Spirit) and Jnana (Knowledge)are not two different things. They are one and the same. That is why the Vedas declared: Satyam, Jnanam, Anantam Brahma (Brahmam is Truth, Wisdom and Infinite). Truth, Wisdom, Infinity and Brahmam are all different names for the Paramatma (Omni-Self). They are synonymous. They are not different from each other.

Jnana and Bhakti lead to the same goal:

What is Jnana? The awareness of Swaswaroopa (one's real nature) is true knowledge. Devotion is the means to achieve oneness with this knowledge (when Self-knowledge becomes one with the Self). Jnana implies freedom from all thoughts. The Jnana-Marga (the path of Knowledge) calls for the control of thoughts by appropriate efforts. Whether one takes to the Jnana-Marga (the path of Knowledge) or the Bhakti Marga (the path of Devotion), the resulting illumination is the same.

For instance, the light of the sun is reflected by the moon. The light from the sun is warm and effulgent. When the same light is radiated by the moon, it is cool and soothing. It is the same light that is present in the sun and the moon. The principle that illumines both the sun and the moon is the Spirit (Atma-Tatwa). The sun's light has been compared to Jnana and the moon's light to Bhakti. Jnana is effulgent, while Bhakti (Devotion) is blissful. Thus Bhakti and Jnana are the beginning and the end of the same process.

God accepts all that comes from a pure heart:

In the phenomenal world, we recognise three entities - Karta, Karma and Kriya (the doer, the act of doing and the goal of the action). This is characteristic of devotion. The Sadhaka (spiritual aspirant) is the Karta (doer). The Sadhana (spiritual exercise) is the Karma (what he does). Getting the vision of the Divine is the Kriya (goal). The same process is described as Jnana (knowledge), Jneya (that which is to be known) and Jnata (the knower). In the highest sense all these are one. They appear in three different, forms at different stages. People are carried away by what they imagine are their spiritual experiences in their Sadhana. But what they should really seek is Anaatma Bhaava (the giving up of the attachment to the non-spiritual). You should not rely on the power and pelf of the world. God accepts only what comes from a pure heart. He does not yield to any mundane offerings. There is a historical illustration for this.

How Shiva accepted Parvati as Ardha:

Both in the Vishnu Purana and the Shiva Purana, Parvati is described as the most beautiful goddess. Conscious of her own exceptional charms, Parvati desired to win Siva as her spouse. But all her efforts proved fruitless. Learning a lesson from this experience and shedding her ego, she embarked on a severe penance. Facing the rigours of heat and cold, wind and rain, she allowed her body to waste away by her penance. Her mind was solely concentrated on Siva. Seeing that she had completely got rid of her ego, Shiva agreed to accept Parvati as Ardhaangini (one half of Himself).

What is the inner meaning of this episode? Nature is symbolic of Parvati. It is exceptionally beautiful. Feeling proud about its charms, it seeks to attract everybody. As it succeeds in its attractions, its ego grows. Man, who is a child of Nature, also develops the ego and leads a life filled with egoism. The ego gets puffed up on the basis of knowledge, physical strength, power and position, handsome looks and such other accomplishments. Even the pride of scholarship takes one away from God.

Persons filled with such conceit can never realise God. Only those free from self-conceit can be God-realised souls. Valmiki, Nanda, Kuchela, Shabari, Vidura, and Hanuman are examples of devotees who realised God, but who could boast of no great lineage, wealth or scholarship. Their supreme quality was freedom from ego. Hanuman, for instance, was content to describe himself as a servant of Rama, despite his great prowess and knowledge. All the accomplishments and acquisitions in this world are transient and impermanent; lured by them, men get inflated and ultimately court ruin. Hence, giving up the notions of one's own doership, man must regard God alone as the doer. He is the giver, He is the recipient and He is also the object that is given.

Time is the very form of God. Birth and death are encompassed by Time. Everyone, therefore, should regard Time as Divine and utilise it for performing sacred actions. You should not waste a single moment. Time wasted is life wasted. The fruits of your actions are determined by Time. All your experiences are the results of your actions, whether it is happiness or sorrow, affluence or poverty. Hence, good and bad depend on what you do. As are your actions, so are the fruits thereof. The way you utilise your time determines the outcome.

God is the origin for all Yugas:

Hence, this new year, which is a form of the Divine, should be put to right use. You have heard about the four aeons called Krita Yuga, Treta Yuga, Dwapara Yuga and Kali Yuga. These are not distinct from each other. The divisions are based on experiences. Whether it be Krita Yuga or Kali Yuga, it has no separate form. According to the conduct of the people at the time, the name is given for the Yuga. Even during Krita Yuga there were people filled with attachments and aversions. There are even in Kali Yuga people wedded to truth and leading virtuous and peaceful lives For all Yugas, God is the origin. Hence one of the names bestowed on God is Yugadi (One from whom the Yuga begins). The Yugadi festival is celebrated for this reason. Everything is a manifestation of the Divine.

Not realising this, man becomes elated when he gets something and feels depressed when he loses something. You should develop the state of equanimity which leaves you unaffected by gain or loss...

Engage yourselves in godly actions:

Atma is Time and Time is God. Therefore, you should not waste time. Fill your time with good actions. There is no greater Sadhana than this. Sanctify the time given to you by good thoughts and good actions. For this, you need to cultivate the company of the good, which will in due course lead you to liberation. Fill your mind with thoughts of God. Engage yourself in godly actions. This is true Sadhana.

People claim to spend hours in meditation. But of what use is it if there is no concentration of mind? It is better if you engage yourself in your regular duties or render social service or participate in Bhajans. By these means try to bring the mind under control. Also, such work will be transformed into worship. Dedicate all your thoughts and actions to God. "Sarva Karma Bhagavat Prityartham" (All actions are done to please God). Then your acts get purified.

If you want to experience God, you have to do it through your duties and actions. This is not so easy. You have been listening to Me for many years. You take down notes and listen to tape records. Has there been the slightest change in you? Such is your life. Only when some change takes place in you, that alone is the fruit of your Sadhana. You go on spending your days and nights in the same routine, but are you making any efforts to sublimate your life? Endeavour to lead an ideal life. In the absence of any change for the better in your daily conduct, all your so called Sadhana (spiritual practices) will be futile.

God resides in the temple of human body:

Jnana is God. Jnana is Atma. Prakriti (Nature) is Jneyam (the thing to be known). Man is a combination of Jnana (God) and Jneyam (Nature). The Bhagavad Gita says that the Kshetra (the field, namely the body) and the Kshetrajna (the knower of the field, namely the Atma) together constitute the human personality Similarly, the scriptures refer to the human body as the temple and the indwelling Spirit as the God installed in that temple. Even a mere intellectual understanding of this fact will make us happy. But we shall be much more happy when we put this understanding into practice in our daily lives. However, it is a pity that we content ourselves with pious resolutions in such matters, without a strong determination to put them into actual practice.

Have your hands in society and heads in forest:

Without the courage of firm conviction and strong determination, no purpose is served by routine Sadhanas undertaken by aspirants who oscillate from moment to moment like the pendulum of a clock. On the contrary, a person who never swerves from his determination even under trying circumstances, is called a Dheera (a hero) and such a person wins the grace of the Lord.

We should try to seek fulfillment in our day-to-day life by basing our mundane activities on spiritual values. As I have been telling you off and on, you must have your hands in the society and head in the forest. That is to say, whatever be the activities with which you are preoccupied in society, you must be steadfast in holding on to the spiritual ideal. This alone is the true Sadhana which will bestow lasting peace on you.

Whatever may be the change in the various Pratibimba (reflections) there will be no change whatsoever in the Bimba (Original). Remember that you are that changeless original - the Atma. All your Sadhanas should be directed towards establishing yourself in this firm conviction and unwavering faith, culminating in your life's fulfillment.

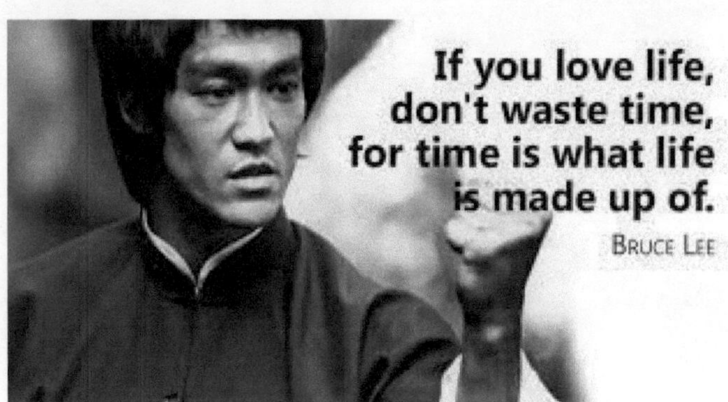

<u>Bhajan and Japa are one and the same:</u>

All your sense organs should be sanctified offering all the actions performed through them as dedication to God.

This is true Bhajan. "Bha" means that which is Bhavyam (sacred or holy). What is Bhavyam? The Atma Tatwa (principle of Atma) which is Divyam (Self-effulgent). The letter "Ja" in the word Bhajan connotes Japa (chanting the Lord's Name). Thus Bhajan and Japa are one and the same.

There is a Japa (which means constant remembrance of God) that goes on incessantly and automatically within you in the breathing process, whatever be the work in which you are engaged. And that is So ham. This is the real Sadhana, because it goes on without any conscious effort on your part, in the same manner as the process of breathing, beating of your heart and circulation of blood within you, which take place without any effort by you. These are all natural processes which go on without any volition on your part. In contrast to this there are some activities which also become involuntary or automatic but because of prolonged practice.

For example, the fingers of one who is in the habit of taking snuff, will unconsciously be moving towards his nose. Similarly, because of habit, some people will be engaged unconsciously in Japa, with their minds wandering somewhere. This is not real Japa. That alone is real Japa which goes on in the super-conscious (but not unconscious) state of mind. Do not entertain any doubt about your ability to reach that stage. You can surely attain that state beyond the shadow of doubt, provided you have a strong determination. Unfortunately, you do not evince such a firm determination and tenacity of purpose in respect of spiritual matters, as you do for the sake of mundane things. Man is prepared to put forth any amount of effort to undertake a journey of millions of miles into outer space but he hardly ever endeavours to go even an inch into his own inner Self. What is the use of all your intelligence and all your worldly acquisitions when they cannot give you Atma Santhi (the untrammelled peace of the Atma). God alone can confer such enduring peace on man.

Therefore, O Embodiments of Divine love! Recognise that the Samvatsara (new year) connotes God who bears several appellations relating to Time. Sanctify the new year by engaging yourselves in pure, selfless and ennobling activities. As far as possible, avoid causing harm or pain to others. As you sow, so you reap. Whenever you feel disturbed by a sense of anger, envy, pride, jealousy and the like, be alert and resort to the contemplation of the Lord.

5 Time Wasters for Youth and How to Deal With Them:

It might be a while before your child understands the value of time, but I'm sure that you've already figured that out. There aren't enough hours in a day, not enough days in a week, and we were all 21 just yesterday.

Unfortunately, those are all lessons we've learned when it's too late. That's why I always try to impress the value of time on all the youth that I coach.

Still, no matter how much they understand what I'm teaching them, it's never easy for kids to appreciate how valuable time is. It's easy for them to spend time in ways that might not only be unproductive, but harmful, too.

As a youth life coach, I encourage parents to think about these five biggest time wasters and how you can deal with them. While reading, keep in mind that these time wasters aren't the end of the world. It's perfectly okay for them to be a part of your child's life, just in moderation.

1. Technology

There's no denying that technology is integrated into our everyday lives, and the same can be said for the lives of kids. Technology connects us, helps us learn and entertains us. You wouldn't be able to read about these time wasters without technology.

But it's easy for people to become obsessed with technology. Some studies have shown that teens spend up to nine hours a day, on average, online. This is mostly on their phone, but could be on tablets, computers, video games or other devices. Technology can be the biggest time waster of any on this list.

What to do about it: Set clear rules around technology use in the house. Define when it can and can't be used. This means that you need to understand technology as well; realize that it's a means of socializing, learning and growing, not just a distraction. Keep that in mind when establishing rules.

2. Procrastination

This might seem like the very definition of wasting time, but procrastination has a cascading impact on how much time it ruins. Procrastination involves starting a task, getting distracted, putting minimal work in, then leaving it until the very last minute.

Not only does this waste multiple chunks of time, but it results in lower-quality results when your child finally crams in the work they need to get done.

What to do about it: The best thing you can do to fight procrastination is get rid of distractions where your kid does their work. By removing these, there are less things to stop your child from working. Figure out how they work best, too, and optimize their workspace for them.

3. Disorganization

Being organized isn't just about keeping up appearances. In fact, keeping a clean room, house and workspace helps kids work more efficiently. But when clutter and messiness overtakes organization, the opposite will happen.

Disorganization leads to increased distractions, difficulty finding things that you need and more stress. All of that adds up to a lot of wasted time.

What to do about it: Make cleaning a regular chore in the house. Youth should be responsible for keeping their own things tidy while assisting at home.

4. Multi-tasking

It might seem like a good idea at first, but it's been proven that multi-tasking doesn't save time and, like procrastinating, ends up with a lesser-quality result. Worse, multi-tasking can easily become frustrating and lead to procrastination.

Even those who feel like they have a grasp of multi-tasking are wasting time when they could be focusing on individual tasks.

What to do about it: Focusing is a championship habit that you should work to develop in your child. Being able to focus on a single task at once and excel at it will pay off later in life. Try to nurture that focus to minimize the time wasted with multi-tasking.

5. Sleeping in

First things first: there is nothing wrong with sleeping in once in a while. In fact, sometimes it's necessary after a long week or when you need to recover.

That being said, it's easy for kids (and adults) to waste their mornings away by sleeping in. Those first few hours of the day can be productive or fun, yet most of us lose them to sleep. Think of all the hours you've lost from an extra thirty minutes of sleep each day that you didn't really need.

Sleeping in and poor sleeping habits can quickly add up to be a major time waster.

What to do about it: Establish a regular sleep routine for your kids. Make sure they're in bed at a reasonable time and aren't staying up on their phone or watching TV. While sleeping in can be a time waster, make sure that your kids are still getting 8-10 hours of sleep; it's just better to sleep 9PM-6AM than it is 2AM-11AM.

Like all bad habits, getting rid of these time wasters won't be easy. But committing to getting some of that time back for you and your family will pay off for everyone involved.

Remember, though, that most of these time wasters are okay in moderation. Be aware of what you need to work on with your child and try to get back some of that lost time.

A Brief Information about Time Waste is Life Waste:

You know, life is really very short. None of us knows when it is time for us go. None of us knows if not today is our very last day on Earth. For some it will be. So how can you be so sure that today is not also your last day on Earth? How can you be so sure that you will still be here tomorrow?

I don't know whether I will still be around tomorrow. I guess so, but I don't know for sure. And neither do you.

Our time on Earth is shortened every moment, whether we like it or not. And once a moment is gone, it is "gone forever." It is deducted from the number of moments we were given when we were born. And with every breath we take, that number shrinks.

Sure, time is an illusion. As Djwal Khul put it, „Time is the sequence of events and of states of consciousness as registered by the physical brain. Where no physical brain exists, what humanity understands by time is nonexistent."

Or, in the words of A Course in Miracles, time is a learning device. So, time is a teaching device which will cease to exist when it is no longer useful in facilitating learning.

Time as we understand it is actually non-existent because the only thing that really exists is the Eternal Now. However, so long as we are working here with time and space, and that applies to all of us here on Earth, the purpose of time and space is to facilitate learning.

Said another way: the little time that is given us is precious. Some peopel like to say: time is money. I like to say: time is Spiritual growth!

Ultimately, we are all eternal, but if we want to break free from the limitations of time and space that we are all caught up in here, then we need to use the precious time that is given us to learn what we have come here to do because, again, the purpose of time is to facilitate learning.

And so I thought today i would just love to lovingly remind all of us that we are here on Earth to learn some lessons.

So many people literally waste their time and their lives. They go from one relationship to the next without learning anything. They waste their life indulging the lower self, reading boulevard magazines to hear the latest gossip, and never close their eyes to go within. Never close their eyes to ask themselves what life is actually all about.

Life is about realizing our divinity. We are here to merge with our Divine Self on Earth and live in love. We are here to be of service to the world. We are here to make the world a better place. We are here to advance humanity to the next higher level of evolution. We are here to be part of the solution, not part of the problem. We are here to transcend the lower self and transcend fear, and not indulge the lower self and buy into fear.

So, don't waste the time that is given you and keep your mind focused on what really matters in life, your Spiritual growth and awakening, and the Spiritual growth and awakening of all of humanity, because at the end of our lives that will be the only thing that will matter anything.

So let's use every moment that is given us wisely. Let's use every moment as a gift and as an opportunity to purify our mind, body and emotions, to render planetary world service and practice the Presence of our Divine Self.

Next time you turn on the TV to watch some nonsense, or buy a boulevard magazine to find out which celebrity got a new haircut or a new lover, or next time you walk over to your neighbor to discuss other people, think twice whether that's really the best way to use your time or if perhaps there is not a better, more constructive way to use the teaching device time whose purpose it is to facilitate learning.

So, always remind yourself that ultimately your life span on Earth is very short. Use every moment of your life wisely to help you realize that you are Divine and so is everyone else! This is the whole purpose of incarnating on Earth.

Quotes:

- If you love life, don't waste time, for time is what life is made up of.

- Lost time is like a run in a stocking. It always gets worse.
- A man who dares to waste one hour of time has not discovered the value of life.
- By doing gossiping we just waste our time and energy as we can utilize our time by spreading some thoughts around people, making them smile, appreciate small

gestures and much more.

- Peaceful protesting against your mind is useless. Unless you are ready to seize control and play like you've got nothing to lose, don't waste your time.

- We live in the midst of plenty but always seem to want more. We feel that we do not have enough time, and yet we waste the precious time we have on video games, text messaging, reading about the lives of talentless celebrities, or earning more money to buy things we don't need.

- Watch less TV and spend less time surfing the web. Cut down on these time wasting activities and replace them with productive activities which will help you realize your financial goals.

- Stop wasting time with trivial matters that don't add value to your life or push you one step closer to your goals.

- Comparing yourself to someone else is a massive waste of time. Steve Errey, The Code of Extraordinary Change

- Time is one of your most valuable commodities and how you spend it determines what your life will be. You can either waste it, invest it or give it away.

- While there are issues that cannot be negotiated or compromised, there are petty things that are not worth getting worked up about. Consider whether something is really worth your time and energy.

- If you worry about something that you have no control over, or can absolutely do nothing about, then you are wasting your time, energy and emotion.

- "I don't dwell in the past; I don't wallow in old events and emotions. I don't waste time on regret. No use going over and over the details of what already happened.
- "Never waste your time it is to precious. There are never any guarantees we will have tomorrow."

- The only person who can derail your productivity plans is you. Don't become your own worst enemy by letting time slip through your fingers.

- Prioritization is a critical aspect of improving our productivity. If we are not productive, then we may not be making the most of the time and energy that we have to get things done.

- The truth is that all of the time in the world is not going to help us if we don't get our lives in order. We need to get our priorities straight, and we need to stop wasting time.

- "Time is also one of the commodities that we can not buy back; we can not exchange anything we possess to trade for time that has been wasted or squandered."
- Time is one of the most precious commodities we have. Each moment is like the water in a river - moving, fluid and never to be experienced again. How you spend your time will be the most important decision you can ever make on earth.

- Are you taking your life for granted? Are you allowing your days to be consumed with boredom and frustration? Time is your most precious gift, not to be dwindled away in idleness or negativity.

- How many things in your life do you do without realizing that they are a waste of time.

- If you want life to roll by without accomplishing anything you want, simply keep throwing your time away. You will never get it back.

- If people would reflect that one can only do one thing at a time and therefore there is never more than one thing to do at a time, there would be less fatigue in the world.
- Time is a decreasing commodity in that we use it up no matter what we do, and it is never given back to you.

- How many things in your life do you do automatically, routinely, that are a waste of time but you don't take the time to remedy them.

- Time = life; therefore, waste your time and waste your life, or master your time and master your life.

- The dying don't tend to waste time talking about trivial things. They realize how precious time is, and most use it as efficiently as possible.

- One thing is for sure, procrastinators waste the most precious asset a human can have.

Time Should Be Used Proper

The proverb time waste is life waste is real. Time is very precious and we should not waste it in any way. Like wise, we can earn the money we spents but we cannot get back the time we have lost. So, this makes the time more valuable than money. Hence, we should utilize the time in the most possible way.

Importance of Time :

The most valuable and precious thing in the world. Also, we should use it for our good as well as for the good of others around us and the society to progress towards a better tomorrow. Moreover, we should teach our children the importance and value of time. Also, wasting time will only lead you to cause an issue to you and the people around you.

Value of Time :

Although most people do not understand how valuable time is until they lost it. By wasting time we can lose valuable thing.

The person who says there is no time is a big fool said by Swami Satya Sai Baba.

Wasting of Time :

What program we see in T.V can be that we were wasting time (or) utilize time. The program which we are watching makes us good mind are not come and wasting time. Other mod of wasting time are 1) sleeping more and talking more in telephone. Swami Satya Sai Baba say that sleeping more (or) sleeping less is not good.

Swami Satya Sai Baba said that television is televisham.

The correct manner is to sleep at a correct time and wakeup at correct time.

Work with a Plan :

We should do work with a plan if not there will be wastage of time what the work we were doing should be planned before and do work at a correct time. By this there will be saving of time Swami Satya Sai Baba told that 6 hours for own work, 6 hours for Devotional work.

Telephone Many members are mis-using telephone.

The matter to speak is 2 min means they were speaking many hours. Many members are using in markets, roads etc., due to this many of accidents were happening. By this more taking than matter there will be wastage of time.

There were you are not the time will not see. The time do it work. The time will not wait for us that we were completed work (or) not. It moves up on without any end.

A time we asked a person to meet and we went late becomes a big mistake. It means you wasted the valuable time of a person. You stealed the time of person.

9 798887 496160

9 798887 496160

Printed by Libri Plureos GmbH in Hamburg,
Germany